RAM AND THE GURU

Written by Bali Rai
Illustrated by Isabelle Duffy

OXFORD
UNIVERSITY PRESS

Words to look out for ...

accuse *(verb)*
accuses, accusing, accused
To accuse someone is to say that they did something wrong.

anticipate *(verb)*
anticipates, anticipating, anticipated
to expect something

compassion *(noun)*
Compassion is care or pity that you show to people or animals that are suffering.

consequence *(noun)*
something that happens as the result of an event or action

deny *(verb)*
denies, denying, denied
to not allow someone to have something

depend *(verb)*
depends, depending, depended
To depend on someone or something is to need them.

instinct *(noun)*
If your instinct is to do something, you can do it without thinking about it and without being told what to do.

participate *(verb)*
participates, participating, participated
To participate in something is to take part in it.

reasonable *(adjective)*
sensible and fair

separate *(adjective)*
apart; not joined to something else

Chapter 1

Every day, Mother sent me to the village well, even though we knew it was waterless. A drought had dried up the river and left the earth dusty and cracked. As a consequence, our crops had not grown. Although we had some grains stored from the previous harvest, they were running out. Our animals were suffering and so were we. I was thirsty, hungry and I did not want to make another pointless trek to the well.

A consequence is something that happens as the result of an event or action.

'You *must* go, Raman,' my mother said. 'There might be water today.'

'There is never any water,' I replied.

This wasn't completely true. One well remained full. It was on a hill, far above the village.

It was owned by a rich, powerful man called Hari, who guarded his well and made us villagers pay to use it. At first, we gave Hari money for the water. In time, just like our food stores, our money began to run out.

Hari had no compassion at all. He simply increased the price. However, we could not hand all our money to him.

I walked to the village well. Several others stood around it, holding buckets. A man attached his bucket to the rope and lowered it down into the darkness. I was twelve years old and had never felt so hopeless.

Compassion is care or pity that you show to people or animals that are suffering.

'Anything today?' asked his wife. Her voice was raspy and dry, as if it had been rolled in the dusty earth. I knew that they had two small children to care for, too. I prayed that they would find some water.

The man shook his head sadly.

I looked up towards the hill. I was sure Hari was up there, sitting by his well, surrounded by guards. I could imagine his sly grin.

'What are we supposed to do?' asked the woman. 'We cannot survive for much longer!'

As I watched an old man count out his last remaining coins so that he could pay for water, my heart broke. I had once believed that all human beings were kind. In times of need, I had assumed that everyone would help one another. Now, as I thought about Hari and his well, I knew I was wrong.

I returned home miserably. Most of us in the village had very little. Yet we never lived separate lives. We always shared what we had. We worked together, and helped each other. We were a real community.

Separate means apart, or not joined to something else.

My mother had taught me to trust in human compassion, and to expect people to be friendly and caring. Now, Hari had changed that.

Compassion is care or pity that you show to people or animals that are suffering.

Our house was a single-storey building made of dried earth blocks and wood, with a thatched straw roof. When I got home, Mother was adding wood to the cooking fire in our little courtyard. She saw how sad I was and took the empty bucket from me. Hari's greed had left me feeling sad and angry.

'Imagine if someone just took water from Hari's well,' I said crossly to her.

'That would be theft,' she replied. 'We are not thieves, Raman.'

'Hari's the thief!' I said. 'Water shouldn't belong to anyone. It's for everyone.'

'I know,' Mother said with a sigh, 'Yet that well is on Hari's land.'

'But he's so greedy,' I told her. 'Why won't he help us?'

Mother thought for a moment. 'Some people don't see the need to help others,' she said. 'Don't worry. Tomorrow, the village elders are gathering some money to buy water from Hari. We'll get by.'

Until the money runs out, I thought.

Chapter 2

The following morning, a village elder called Mata collected money from every family that was able to participate. The elders were people who had lived in the village for a long time and were trusted to make fair and wise decisions.

After collecting the money, Mata, two male elders and several older children carried buckets and clay pots up the hill. I went with them, keen to help.

I felt proud that we were all coming together.

Two guards stood by the well. They grinned when they saw us.

'Wait here!' said one. 'I'll get Hari.'

Hari came out of his house a few moments later, eating a juicy slice of mango. He had fine silk clothes, a gold chain around his neck, and dazzling shiny rings on his fingers.

To participate in something is to take part in it.

'I knew you'd be back,' Hari snarled.

'You are cruel,' said Mata, bravely accusing him to his face. 'Yet you were such a sweet child, Hari. Don't you remember? How did such a kind boy become so mean?'

For a brief moment, I thought I saw a trace of regret on Hari's face.

To accuse someone is to say that they did something wrong.

'I'm not cruel,' he said. 'I have been more than reasonable. However, I am a businessman. I cannot give things away for free.'

'Pah!' burst out Mata. 'You don't own water. It belongs to us all! You're a spoilt child who inherited his father's wealth and land.'

'Yet here you are,' Hari replied. 'Standing here with your dusty coins, begging me for water. Perhaps this time I'll say no.'

'Please!' begged Preet, one of the male elders. 'We need the water.'

A reasonable person is sensible and fair.

'Pay my men and take some,' said Hari coldly, turning back to his house.

One by one, we filled the buckets and clay jars with water. On the way home, I walked with my friend Dev.

Dev was the same age as me, but taller and broader in the shoulders. The water was heavy, but he carried a bucket in each hand.

'Maybe we should just *take* the water?' I suggested.

Dev gave me a smile. 'You know,' he replied, 'I was thinking the same thing ...'

Together we worked out a plan. It was one that might get us into trouble, but we were determined to try it.

Chapter 3

That evening, I waited for Mother to fall asleep. Then I crept out of the house, taking my water bucket with me.

The Moon lit my way as I left the village to meet Dev by Hari's hill. He waited with two more wooden buckets.

'Are you scared?' he asked.

'A little,' I replied.

'Me too,' said Dev. 'But the village is suffering.'

He was right. We could not allow it to continue. We had do what little we could. We couldn't help everyone just yet, but our three buckets of water would be a good start.

We had cooked up our plan on the walk back from Hari's. Now, we were going back for more water. Only this time, we wouldn't pay him a single rupee.

If we were caught, we'd be in serious danger.

'I hope the guards are asleep,' said Dev.

We climbed the hill warily, making sure we couldn't be seen or heard. When we reached Hari's land, we stopped to take a breath.

'Ready?' I asked.

Dev nodded, and we crept forward. There was no turning back now.

The guards slept on woven mats, close to the well. At rest, they didn't seem so scary, but if they woke up …

I held a finger to my lips. 'Careful,' I whispered to Dev.

We edged towards the well, eager to get our task done quickly. The sooner we left, the better. Dev attached his first bucket to the rope. Then he lowered it down into the well. The handle creaked a little, but not enough to wake the guards.

'Slowly,' I told him.

Dev managed to raise his bucket of water without making another sound. He set it down, and then it was my turn.

I tied my bucket and began to lower it. I worked slowly and surely, eager not to alert the sleeping guards. Suddenly, the handle got stuck and the bucket would not move.

I put more effort into turning the handle, but nothing happened. I tried again and it started to groan, creak and squeal.

'What is going on?' a guard bellowed. Both men jumped to their feet.

'*Run!*' I shouted, grabbing Dev's arm.

'What about the water?' he asked.

'Leave it!' I replied. 'We have to go!'

The guards roared in rage and chased after us as we crashed through Hari's gate and back towards the path. Just then, the Moon disappeared behind a cloud.

'I can't see anything!' Dev cried out.

'Just stay behind me!' I yelled in reply.

I knew the hill path well and used my instinct to guide me. The men were close behind, but one of them stumbled.

'They're slowing down!' Dev shouted.

'Don't look back at them!' I told him. 'Just concentrate on me!'

At the bottom of the hill, I realized the guards had stopped chasing us. We paused and took deep breaths.

If your instinct is to do something, you can do it without thinking about it and without being told what to do.

My lungs burned from the effort.

'That was too close!' Dev panted, his hands on his knees.

'We didn't get any water,' I pointed out. 'We failed.'

I saw a figure shuffling towards us, carrying a flaming torch. From the light of the flame, I recognized Mata. My stomach churned.

'We're in big trouble,' said Dev.

Mata glared at us. 'What have you done?' she asked, her eyes wide with anger.

I glanced at Dev and decided I would take the blame to protect him. He didn't need to face the consequences too.

'I wanted to help the village,' I replied. 'I asked Dev to come with me.'

'Help?' asked Mata. 'In what way?'

'We were going to take some water,' I explained. 'Then no one would have to pay Hari.'

Mata shook her head. 'When he finds out, he will deny us any more water,' she replied.

My face grew hot. I felt terrible.

Mata placed a hand on my arm, her expression softening. 'I know you were trying to help, Raman,' she said.

A consequence is something that happens as a result of an event or action.

If you are denied something, you are not allowed to have it.

Sighing deeply, Mata continued. 'You should have come to me first. Or asked your mother. We <u>depend</u> on that water.'

I looked at my feet. 'Mother said taking the water would be theft,' I replied.

'She knew?' asked Mata.

'No,' I said quickly. 'I only asked why we didn't just take the water.'

'Oh, Raman,' said Mata.

She turned to Dev. He looked away as well.

'Come on,' she said. 'Time you two went home.'

We walked to Dev's house and then Mata took me home. Her grey cat appeared from some bushes and meowed at us.

To <u>depend</u> on someone or something is to need them.

'There, there, dear one,' Mata said. 'No need to complain. I'll feed you when we get back.'

I remembered the conversation between Mata and Hari. 'Did you know Hari when he was younger?' I asked.

Mata looked thoughtful, as though she was remembering something sad. 'I knew his entire family,' she said. 'His parents were kind and decent.'

'And Hari was different?'

'He inherited his parents' house and land,' she explained. 'But he isn't like them. Money has gone to his head. He thinks himself better than us.'

Mata stopped outside my house.

'Hari lost his wife, too,' she said. 'Afterwards, he became angry and cruel. He's never got over her passing.'

I suddenly felt sad for Hari. Yet none of that excused his cruelty.

'Maybe we can talk to him?' I suggested. 'Tell him we understand why he's so angry.'

Mata shook her head. 'I've tried many times,' she said. 'He doesn't listen.'

The night air was warm and insects buzzed all around us. I said goodbye to Mata.

'I'm afraid your actions will mean trouble,' she said, 'but I will support you.'

As Mata left, her grey cat stood with me for a while, until it spotted a rat. Suddenly, it bolted into some bushes.

I looked up at the hill, wondering if Hari ever felt bad. Or did he sleep soundly, without a care in the world?

It didn't matter either way. My actions had probably just made things worse.

Chapter 4

In the morning, I made another pointless trek to the village well. I wondered if anyone knew what Dev and I had done. At least the guards hadn't recognized us in the darkness. Still, I felt bad, which made me hot and grumpy.

When I saw Dev I wondered if he felt the same. He had some different news, however.

'There are two strangers in the village square,' Dev told me. 'A wise man and his follower. They are sitting on the floor, meditating.'

'Why are they here?' I asked.

'My father said they're famous,' replied Dev. 'They have been travelling all over the country. The wise man is said to be a great teacher.'

What sort of teacher? I wondered.

A crying woman approached us. Mata and some others were with her.

'We went to buy water from Hari,' she sobbed. 'Last night, someone tried to steal from his well. He refused to sell us any more water.'

My heart sank as I glanced at Dev.

'What have we done?' Dev whispered.

'This is a calamity!' said an elder. 'Who are these thieves?'

I began to step forward, but Mata's eyes grew wide and she shook her head.

Mata took my arm. 'Let us go and see this wise man,' she suggested. 'Perhaps he can help us.'

'I feel awful,' I told her as we set off.

'You should,' she replied. 'Yet there's no point in worrying now. We must do something about it.'

The strangers were meditating when we arrived. One had a pointed beard and wore an orange turban. He was playing an unfamiliar string instrument.

The other man's turban was rounder and smaller, and he wore plain clothes made from simple fabric. He sat cross-legged with his eyes closed and chanted the same words again and again.

I watched and listened for a short while, and then the men stood up. Mata approached one of the men and I spoke to his friend with the instrument.

'Welcome,' I said. 'I am Raman.'

'And I am Mardana,' he replied warmly. I asked him what his instrument was.

'This is called a *rabab*,' he said.

The wooden *rabab* had a long, narrow neck and a wide body. It also had strings that made pleasingly rich notes when plucked, some sharp and short, others soft and drawn out. I could have listened to it all day.

'Thank you for your welcome,' said Mardana.

'Who is that man you're with?' I asked.

'His name is Nanak,' Mardana told me. 'He is the wisest human being I have ever met. We are travelling the land, teaching people.'

'What is it you teach?'

''We teach that God is in every living thing and that all humans and all animals are therefore equal.'

'I wish that were true,' I said. I thought about Hari and his well.

'I believe it to be true,' he told me.

Just then, Nanak joined us. He had a friendly face. I liked him immediately.

'Mata tells me your village needs water,' Nanak said.

I nodded. 'Then she told you about Hari, too,' I said.

'Indeed,' Nanak replied, 'and about your attempt to help the village.'

I looked away, feeling bad.

'Helping others is important,' Nanak continued. 'But you must not steal.'

'I just wanted to do something,' I replied, still unable to look at him.

'I understand,' said Nanak. 'Maybe we can fix this problem.'

Nanak asked me to take him and Mardana to Hari's house.

'Of course,' I replied. 'Although he won't listen.'

'We can try,' said Nanak.

Chapter 5

I led the way up the path, towards Hari's house. The first section was easy but then it grew steeper. We villagers were used to it.

'This climb better be worth it,' muttered Mardana.

'It's not so bad,' I told him.

'Tell that to my aching feet,' Mardana complained. 'Nanak and I have walked for many hundreds of miles since we began our journey.'

Hari's guards were waiting for us at the top.

'Go away,' one of them snarled.

'Please tell your master that we have come for water,' said Nanak.

The guard grinned. 'You villagers are not allowed any water,' he said. 'Not after trying to steal it.'

'You don't seem to understand,' Nanak replied. 'We need water. Please fetch your master. I am sure he will listen to us.'

'Get lost!' the guard shouted. 'Before I throw you back down the hill!'

We left empty-handed. At the bottom of the hill, we sat and rested. I felt terrible that my actions had made things worse for the village. Mata was right. Hari was angry now: there would be no more water for us.

Nanak stood up.

'I think Hari deserves a second chance,' he said. 'Come on.'

'Why?' I asked. 'He won't change his mind.'

'People deserve a chance to change their ways,' Nanak replied. 'We may be lucky this time. We cannot know unless we try.'

Chapter 6

Off we went for the second time. This time Hari was waiting, too. He glanced at me, before glaring at Nanak and Mardana.

'You must be the one they call Guru Nanak,' said Hari. 'People in the city talk about you.'

'I am,' said Nanak.

'You teach people that everyone is supposedly equal,' said Hari.

Nanak smiled. 'We *are* equal,' he replied. 'For God is within everyone and everything.'

'If that's so, then why are you begging for my water?' asked Hari.

'I am asking because you have water,' said Nanak. 'And I have none.'

'That proves you are not my equal,' Hari replied.

I was getting angry. I wanted to shout at Hari, but I managed to keep calm.

'Will you give us water?' asked Mardana.

'Ah, the silent one speaks,' said Hari. 'The man who follows his master like an obedient dog.'

'He is not my master,' Mardana replied. 'He is my teacher – my guru. There is a difference. A guru earns respect through kindness and wisdom. A master rules through greed and fear.'

Hari was annoyed by Mardana's words. 'The answer is still no,' he said.

We left without water, again.

Back in the village, my feet ached, and I was thirsty. We shared a small amount of the precious water that Mother had saved. Nanak was lost in thought.

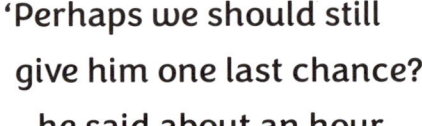

'Perhaps we should still give him one last chance?' he said about an hour later.

'What is the point?' asked Mardana.

'I can go alone, if you'd like,' Nanak replied.

I jumped to my feet. I had caused enough problems in trying to steal Hari's water.

'I can't let you go back alone,' I said. 'It's my fault he's so angry.'

So, off we went again.

Hari saw us coming and groaned.

'Back so soon?' he said, laughing at us.

This time, I could not hold my temper.

'Would your parents have wanted you to be this way?' I snapped.

Hari stopped laughing. His eyes bulged and his face filled with rage.

'Do not mention my parents!' he yelled.

'And your wife?' I continued. 'What would your family say if they could see you now? The village is suffering. Show some compassion!'

Compassion is care or pity that you show to people or animals that are suffering.

'Get them!' Hari commanded his guards.

We ran down the hill to escape them. I was annoyed and sad when we got back to the village. I don't know why I had anticipated that Nanak could change Hari. Not even he could melt Hari's stone-cold heart.

'What now?' I asked.

'It's time to meditate and call God's name,' said Nanak.

He saw a short stick and picked it up. 'I wonder ...' he said.

Then he sat cross-legged and began to chant, with Mardana listening beside him. He seemed to enter a dream state, shutting out the world around him. His eyes were closed and soon he was in a trance.

To anticipate something is to expect it.

Chapter 7

My mother and Mata were sitting in the shade under some trees. I went to join them.

'Where have you been?' Mother asked.

'We went to ask Hari to change his mind,' I replied. 'I was the one who tried to steal his water.'

'Raman!' exclaimed my mother.

'Don't be too hard on him,' said Mata. 'He was just trying to help.'

'*You* knew?' my mother asked Mata.

'Yes,' the elder replied.

'I'm sorry,' I said, feeling sad. 'Hari didn't listen to Nanak either.'

'He won't listen to anyone,' Mata sighed.

I glanced at Nanak. His eyes were still closed and now he was chanting. He was using the stick he'd found to dig a small hole in the dry earth. I went for a closer look. Mardana saw me approaching them.

'Sssh,' he whispered to me. 'Do not disturb him.'

After a few moments, Nanak opened his eyes, but he seemed unhappy with his work. He repeated the process several times. Each time, he looked unhappy with the results.

'Maybe I need to be closer to the hill,' he said suddenly.

He moved towards the hill, where he sat by the path and began to chant again. Soon, he was scratching the earth there too. I went nearer and saw something happening. The dirt grew darker as he scraped at it.

Suddenly, a gush of water burst to the surface. Nanak opened his eyes, saw what had happened, and smiled.

'Thank you,' he said, before continuing to chant.

I could not believe my eyes. The gush of water grew stronger and stronger. It was a spring!

Chapter 8

'*Water!*' I yelled. 'He's found water!' Mata and my mother rushed over. Mardana was right behind them. They were as stunned as I was.

'We are saved!' cried Mata.

'How is this possible?' asked my mother. 'This is a miracle!'

Soon others heard, and ran up in delight to see the spring for themselves.

'A miracle!' they shouted. 'The guru has saved us all!'

The village elders gathered. They shook their heads in amazement. How had the guru discovered water?

Nanak closed his eyes again and continued chanting.

Moments later I heard a rumble like distant thunder. *How can it be thunder?* I thought. *The rainy season is nowhere near. If it's not thunder …*

'*Boulder!*' Mardana shouted. '*Run!*'

I looked up and saw a massive rock rolling towards us along the path. Then time seemed to slow down.
My first thought was for my mother. I saw her pulling Mata to safety, out of the boulder's path. The other villagers scattered. I could feel my heart pounding.

I turned back to Nanak.

Nanak hadn't moved. He hadn't even opened his eyes at the panic surrounding him. He remained where he was, chanting.

Soon the boulder would smash directly into him.

'*Guru-Ji!*' I yelled. '*Move!*'

It was too late to do anything. Then Nanak held up his right hand.

I could not watch this wise and kind man be crushed to death. I closed my eyes ...

And nothing happened. No shouting or screaming. Just silence. Hardly daring to breathe, I opened my eyes ... but Nanak had not moved.

The boulder had stopped completely. Nanak held it back, his hand imprinted on the rock's surface. How could this be?

That was when I saw Hari. He was running down the track and I could tell he was stunned. He bumped into me and we both stood staring at Nanak.

'He's alive!' said Hari. 'I thought that …'

Nanak opened his eyes, turned to us, and smiled gently.

Hari knelt before Nanak and bowed.

'I sent that boulder crashing towards you,' he whispered. 'Then I realized Raman was right. My parents and wife wouldn't have wanted this. I do not want this. You've performed a great miracle, wise Guru. I beg your forgiveness.'

Nanak put a hand on Hari's arm.

'You are forgiven,' he said. Listen to God, who lives within you. Then you will see the way forward and make your wrongs right.'

Nanak and Mardana stayed for two months and I spent a lot of time talking with them. I began to practise what they taught me. I wasn't the only one. Hari joined me in learning from Guru Nanak.

Soon, Hari too was following Nanak's teachings.

The boulder never moved again. It stayed by the spring, complete with Nanak's handprint. Each year, many people visited this wonder. They had heard of Nanak's miracle and wanted to see it for themselves. Many had become followers of his teachings. *Sikhs*, they called us. Students of Guru Nanak.

About Guru Nanak

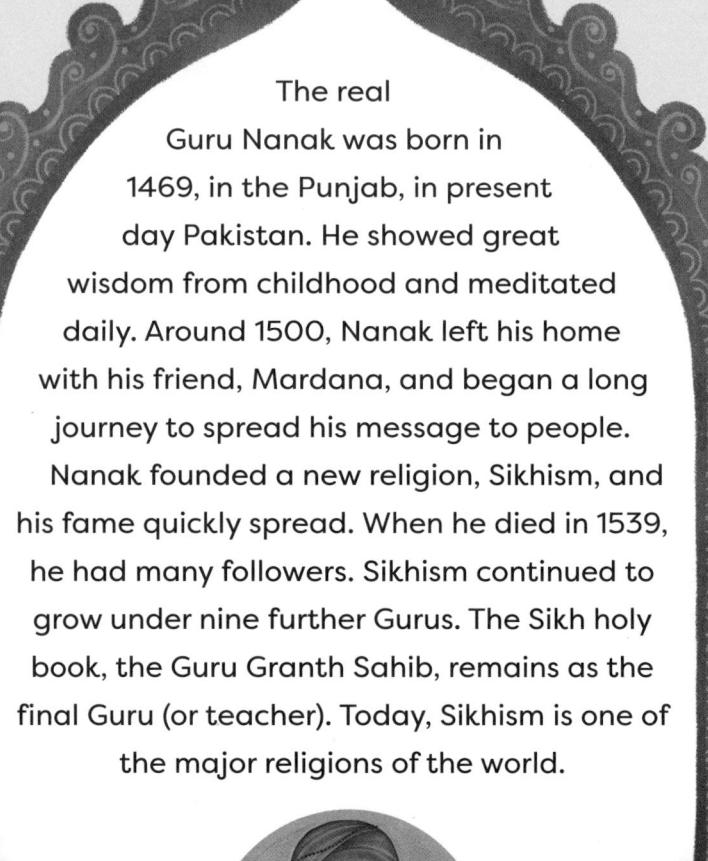

The real Guru Nanak was born in 1469, in the Punjab, in present day Pakistan. He showed great wisdom from childhood and meditated daily. Around 1500, Nanak left his home with his friend, Mardana, and began a long journey to spread his message to people. Nanak founded a new religion, Sikhism, and his fame quickly spread. When he died in 1539, he had many followers. Sikhism continued to grow under nine further Gurus. The Sikh holy book, the Guru Granth Sahib, remains as the final Guru (or teacher). Today, Sikhism is one of the major religions of the world.